TABLE OF CONTENTS

INTRODUCTION

Skills are often seen as endowments and not necessarily acquired through formal or informal exposure.this is erroneous.everyone has the potential for all skills because GOD does not discriminate in bestowing his wisdom on men,however,skills for operation are largely learnt especially high level skills needed to command significant attentions.

This is why one finds that in the world in the 21st century products and services needed by the common man are provided by semi illiterate or completely unschooled people who managed to acquire some skills.

Everyone can make income from acquiring skills

You don't need an office job to make extra income

CHAPTER 1

HANDMADE BAGS

Handbags

A handbag,also referred to as a purse,pocket book or pouch in American English,is a medium to large bag that is often fashionable, designed and typically used by women to hold personal belongings.

The terms ''purse''and handbag are often used interchangeably,however,unlike purse.which originally referred to a small bag for holding coins,a handbag is a large needed accessory, that holds items beyond currency, such as Women's personal items and emergency survival items.

Handbags have been around for many years and have been used by both men and women as fashion accessories as well as functional ones.they come in variety of shapes,colors and sizes; and they are made from a wide variety of materials ranging from cloth to leather and synthetic materials e.t.c.A handbag may be close able by a zipper ,stud(kissing lock)or simply by folding.

In the 18th and 19th centuries,men's demands for handbags dropped due to the introduction of pockets in their trousers.Women on the other hand have shown a strong demand for larger handbags that carry more items for everyday use.

In the modern world,handbags have become very fashionable among young men and women,particularly students.A visit to any institution of higher learning will reveal a wide array of handbags ,uniquely designed and sometimes customized to meet individuals' needs and tastes.

We have different types of handbags we can make with crafts and arts

TOTE BAGS

These are medium to large bags with two straps and an open top,often used for shopping,just like the satchel tote bags has a wide flat bottom with which it can rest on the ground

These bags are handmade bags that anyone can produce and sell..
I have sold a couple in the last few months. This can be used as a
side business to make extra income
It doesn't have to be perfect just try and make it presentable, I prefer
colorful bags

SIMPLE STEPS ON HOW TO MAKE A TOTE BAG

 This step by step will walk you through the super easy process of
making a tote bag. This particular variation is a pretty heavy duty
one, so feel free to adjust a bit if you don't need one that will carry
such a heavy load.

You will need:
- Sewing machine. The walking foot machine at any Techshop
location is a great bet, but any machine will do.
You can equally use needles and thread for those who don't have
sewing machine
- Canvas or some similar woven fabric. Canvas is cheap and pretty
tough so that was my choice. My bottom is
made of waxed canvas to make it a bit water proof and extra
rugged, but we will cross that bridge when we get
to it.
- Webbing, enough to go up both sides, and make the handles at
the very least. You can figure this by
multiplying the height of your bag by 4 and adding 2-4 ft depending
on how big you want the handles and if you
want to wrap the webbing all the way under the bag (extra
reinforcement).

This is a pretty basic project so I would say give yourself an hour
and half to two hours tops.

Materials Needed:
1/2 yard cotton fabric
1/2 yard of complementary cotton fabric for inner lining

1/2 yard of heavy fusible interfacing
42" of canvas strap
fabric scissors or rotary cutter
sewing machine
thread
iron
You can make something like this

1. Cut Fabrics

For the first part of this DIY tote bag project, cut two 18"x14" rectangles of both outer and inner fabric choices then cut two 18"x14" rectangles of interfacing. Cut canvas straps into two 21" lengths.

2. Snip Corners

On the long side of all rectangles, snip a 2"x2" square from only the bottom corners. Repeat for interfacing. This will form the base of the tote.

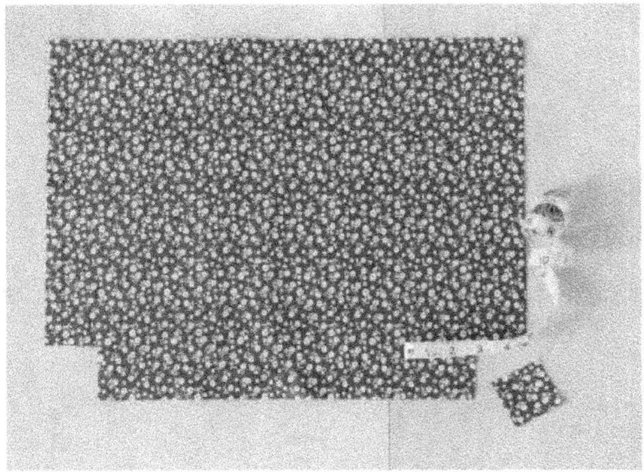

Add Interfacing and Sew Sides

Press interfacing to the wrong side of the outer fabric rectangle. Tip: Follow the manufacturer's directions for heating and adhering your interfacing. Pin outer fabric's right sides together and sew straight 1/2" seams along the sides and bottom of the piece. Note: Leave the top and two clipped corners unsewn. Press seams open.

4. Create Corners

Pinch together gaps in snipped corners, lining up the side and bottom seams in the center. Pin straight across and sew a 1/2" seam. This step adds depth to the bag and creates a flat bottom.

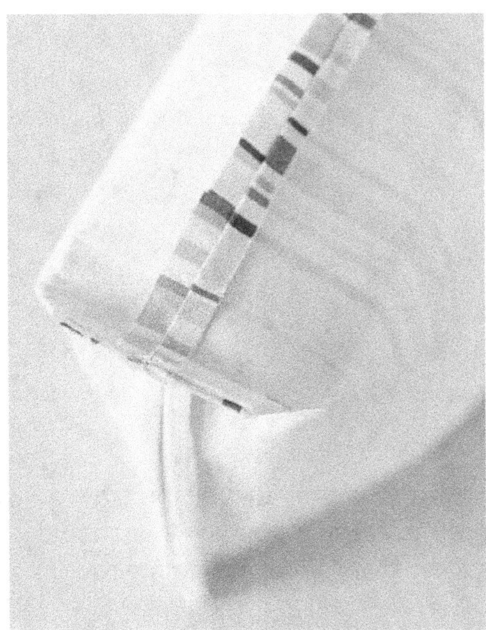

5. Sew Liner Sides and Corners

Pin right sides of inner (liner) fabric rectangles together and repeat the above steps.

6. Piece Together and Pin

Flip liner right-side out and place inside outer fabrics so that right sides are together. Tuck canvas straps between inner and outer fabrics so that two edges of one face the front and two edges of the other face the back of bag. Pin the end of each canvas strap approximately four inches from side seam then pin fabric edges together around perimeter of bag opening.

7. Sew Bag Opening

Beginning at a side seam, stitch a 1/2" seam almost all the way around the tote, stopping 4" before the starting point — this should catch all four ends of the canvas straps while leaving ample room for turning.

8. Turn and Press

Pull both fabrics and straps through the 4" gap, turning the tote bag right-side out. Lightly press with a warm iron to remove wrinkles.

9. Top-Stitch and Finish

Top-stitch around the tote bag's entire opening to finish edges. This will also help reinforce canvas straps and shut the gap left in the previous step for turning.

Steps on how you can make any other bags of your choice

- step one choose any type of fabric that you desire to make know if
the bag will be carrying heavy items eg. books so you can go for
heavy or stronger material because a lighter fabric would rip if it tries
to carry something heavy
Do a proper measurement before you start

For the top edge of the fabric down by 1 inch using a straight pin to
keep the fold in place repeat the order rectangle so daddy hem we
will be the same on both pieces
Use a sewing machine to create a straight stitch one and half inch
below the folded edge of the fabric on both rectangle
If you want to make a Lined bag,lay the lining rectangle on top of
the rectangle out of fabric by folding the edges down together are
using a straight pin to keep in place and then sew the pieces
together with a straight stitch so the two rectangle together by
placing the hemmed rectangle back to back so that's the wrong side
of the fabric are facing out
sew along the sides and bottom using straight stitches
Mitre each bottom corner folding the bag so that instead of coming
together at a 90 degree angle the bottom and side seam are
stacked on top of one another and sew across the corner keeping
the new steam perpendicular to the existing stems

Repeat the process on the other corner and when you flip the bag right side out the corner will be blunted

Making a handle

Depending on the bag you are making

 measure 2 inches wide strips of the fabric and cut two equal length from the fabric

fold each strips in half so that the inside of the fabric faces outward and use an iron to press and hold it together

Sew the long edges together by using his sewing machine to make a straight stitch along the long edges of both handle

Turn the handle right side out and flatten the handle with an iron

Fold the end of your handle under by half inch and Iron them to create a crease and place the ends over the marks you made to show where the handle should be

Top stitch a square onto the overlapping handle fabric to hold its firmly in place

CHAPTER 2

BEAD MAKING

Bead making or bead work is the act or craft of making things with beads. Beads can be woven together with specialized threads such as fishing lines or flexible wire

A bead is a small, decorative object that is formed in a variety of shapes and sizes of a material such as stone, bone, shell, glass, plastic, wood or pearl and with a small hole for threading or stringing. Beads range in size from under 1 millimetre (0.039 in) to over 1 centimetre (0.39 in) in diameter.

Beads may be classified into several types based on the materials used in making them some examples of beads include sand beads, crystal beads, plastic beads, pipe beads

SAND BEADS

Sand cast beads are also referred to as powdered glass beads and feature glass beads crafted by hand. These beads were popularly used as currency during trade in West African countries such as Ghana.

These beads are made in a process where bead makers grind up bottles or other scrap glass to produce recycled beads. These are then fired in clay molds at a relatively low temperature in order to give the beads texture.

Sand cast beads are available in beautiful colors such as blue and may be strung bead to bead to produce beautiful strands on raffia.

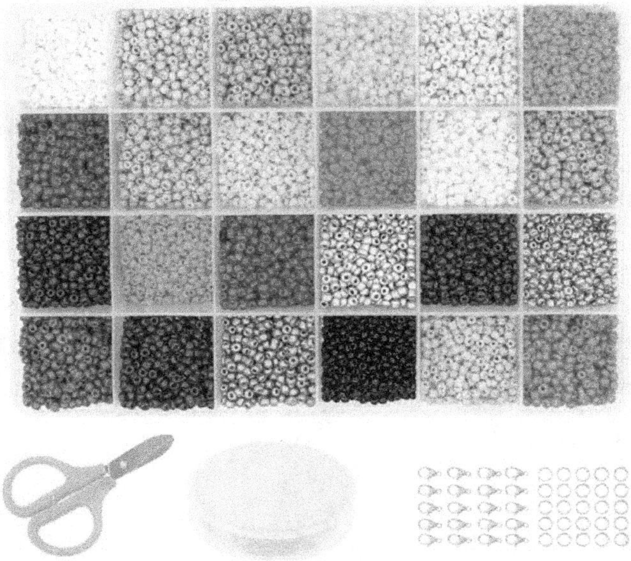

CRYSTAL BEADS

Crystals are crystal beads made out of leaded glass and have a high shine. They are usually faceted for additional shine. The most commonly known crystals are Swarovski Elements but there are Czech crystals too which are of good quality at a cheaper price.

PLASTIC BEADS

Plastic. Many plastic beads are made using a technique similar to the one used to create their glass counterparts. Colored liquid plastic is poured into molds and left to harden. These beads are cheap and cheerful and are great for kids to work with

PIPE BEADS

Pipe beads are used to create intricate embroidery designs and jewellery strands. They are made by cutting glass tubes in imported machines in long cylindrical shapes. The sizes available in pipe seed beads are 4.5 millimetres, 6.0 millimetres, 9.0 millimetres, 25 millimetres sizes.

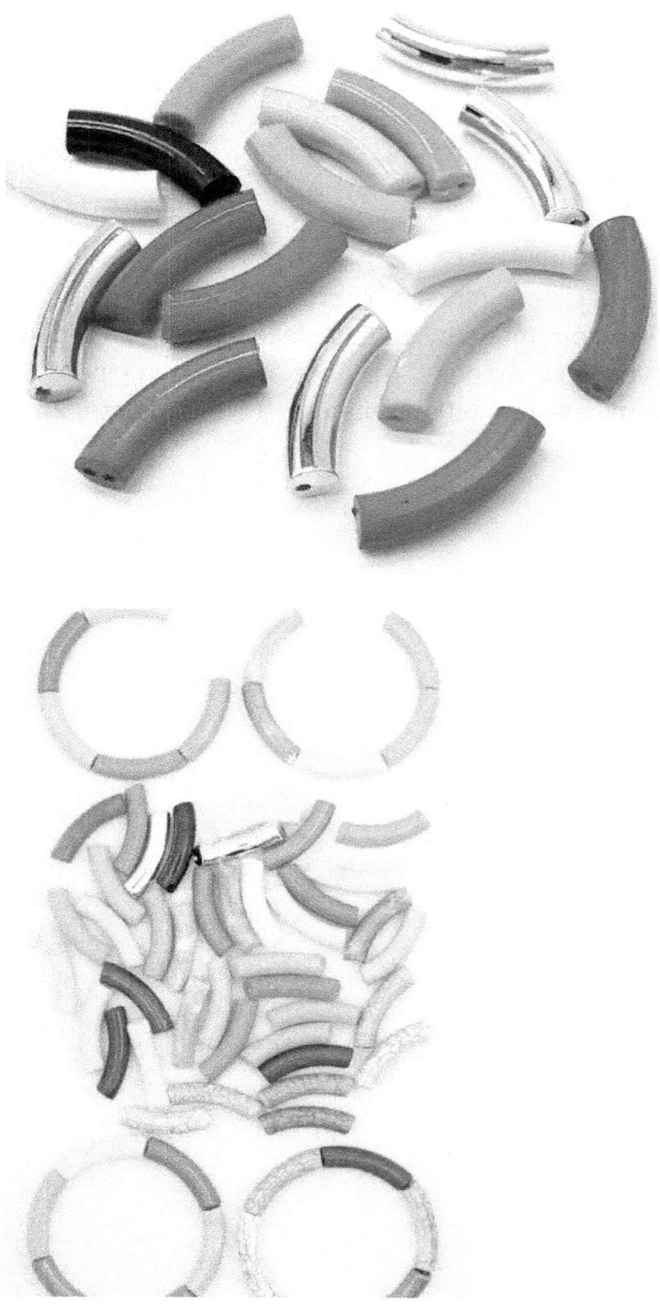

Tools for bead making

Fish line

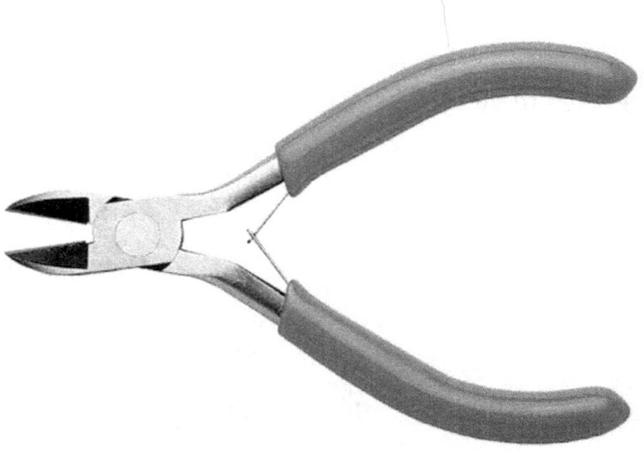

Wire cutter

Beads

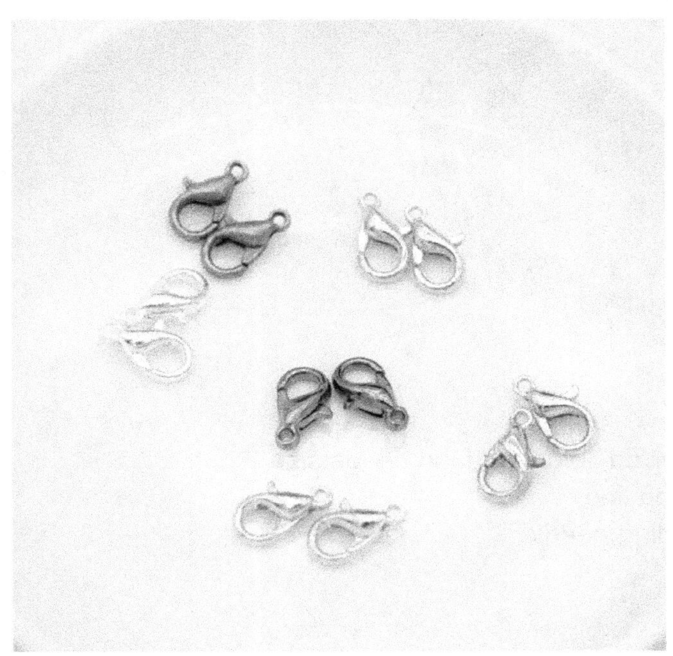

Hooks

How to make Spiral Necklace

Materials
Choose your preferred colors of sand beads size 2
Size 0.30mm fishing line
Size 11 or 12 beading needle

Procedure
Step1: cut a comfortable length of fishing line
Step2: thread one sand bead, this will act as your temporary
Stopper it will be removed at the end of the work.pass the line over
it again to keep it intact
Step3: if you are using multiple colors first thread 4 dormant color
followed by 4 active colors making a total of eight beads
Step4: pass the needle through the first four beads which are the
dormant color
Step5: Thread 1 dormant color and 4 active colors beads
Step6: pass the needle through the last 3 dormant beads and the
new one you just added
Step7: repeat step 5 and 6 until you get your desired length
Step8: attach your hook

ABUJA CONNECTION

3 mm monofilament (its length will depend on the piece of jewelry you're making)

2 types of beads of your choice, one is smaller and one is bigger
(for this tutorial – 6 mm rotelle crystals and 11/o seed beads)
Clasps

And these are the steps Abuja connection bead making consists of:

1) Cut a thread and tie each end to needles

2) Put 3 bigger beads in the middle of the thread, then put one more
of them through one needle and pull the second needle through it.
You will get a cross-shaped form.

3) Put 10 smaller beads on each side of this cross

4) Take 1 bigger bead and again pull both needles through it

5) Put one bigger bead on each side, then again pull both needles
through one more bigger bead. This will be your main element of the
jewelry. Repeat previous steps until you get the length you need for
your piece of jewelry.

6) Now it's time to add more levels. Put 2 bigger beads on the right
side and one on the left

7) Pull the right needle through the left single bead. To begin the
second layer, put two bigger beads on the right side and one on the
left side. Pull the right needle through the left bead. This will make a
turn and allow you to begin the second layer. For the first element of
the new layer use 6 smaller beads on the left side and 7 smaller
beads on the right.

8) After each central bead, pull a needle through the central bigger
bead of the previous level. You will need one bigger bead less since
the bead from the previous level will be a part of the cross

9) You can add the third level to the second or just add it to a new thread

10) In the end, put 8 smaller beads on one side, then pull the second needle through them in the opposite direction. Pass both needles through the top two bigger beads. Make some knots and cut the thread, apply the clasps. Your beaded jewelry is ready!Abuja connection bead making

2. New Abuja Connection Bead Tutorial
Steps on how to make Abuja connection beads are generally similar for both old and new styles. The only difference lies within the main element of the chain. The materials you need are the same. Here is how to make Abuja connection a bead in new style:

1) Put one bigger bead in the middle of the thread, then put 5 smaller beads on each side of it.

2) But one more bigger bead, then pull the needle from the opposite side through it. That's basically it – this is the main element for the new Abuja connection bead, repeat the same steps as for the previous tutorialSteps on how to make Abuja connection bead

HIDDEN TREASURE

Hidden treasure necklace are often made out of expensive crystal beads. It comes along with earrings and bracelets
Materials
Size 6 crystal beads (stone bead)
Size 2 sand beads
Size 0.30mm fishing line
Size 11 or 12 beading needle and hook
Procedure
Step1: Cut a comfortable length of fishing line then fix your needle
Step2: pick one sand bead and one crystal beads beach each 3 times such that you have 6 beats on the line
Step3: pass the needle through the first sand beads to form a circle
Step4: Pass 5 Sand Beads and pass the needle through the next Sand Bead
Step5: pick another five Sand Bead and pass the needle through the next Sand Bead in between the Crystal Bead
Step6: Pick 5 Sand Bead and pass the needle through the last sand bead and extra 3 sand beads
Step7: Pick 1 crystal beads and pass the needle through 6th Sand Bead
Step8: repeat step 4-7 until you get your desired length
Step9: attach hook

ST PETERSBURG STITCH

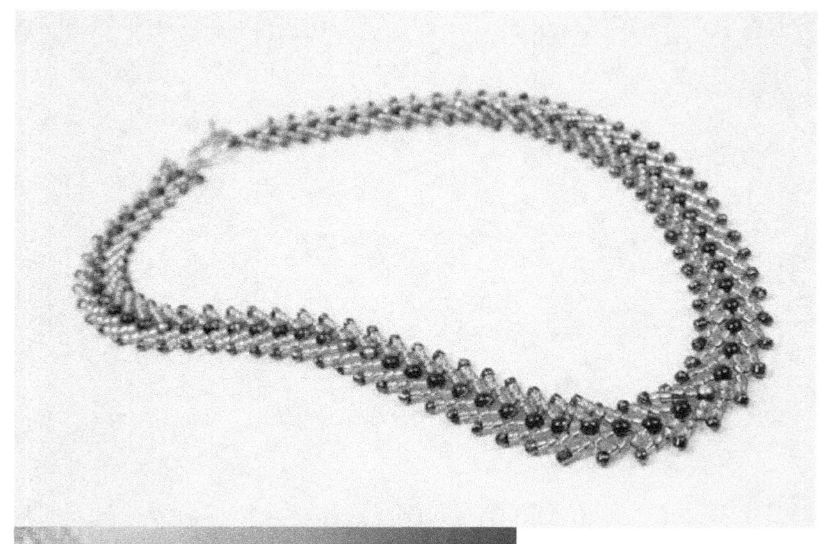

Materials List

size 11/o seed beads
size D beading thread
beading needle

Instructions
Step-by-Step Instructions

Attach a stop bead to the thread, leaving an 8 inch tail. Pick up 6 seed beads, and slide them down to the stop bead.

Stitch back up through the center 2 beads again, and carefully pull snug to form a P-shaped cluster.

Pick up 1 seed bead. Stitch back down through the top three beads of the column that your thread is exiting – the long side of the P. Pull snug to lock the new bead into place at the top.

Pick up 1 bead and stitch up through the two beads of the short side of the P. Pull snug to lock the new bead into place.

Pick up 4 seed beads and slide them down to the beadwork.

Stitch up through the 1st 2 beads picked up again, and carefully pull snug to form a new P shape branching off from the first. To help keep tension, use your off hand to push the new beads towards the beadwork as you pull the thread tight.

Repeat steps 2-4 until your chain reaches the desired length.

Finish chain as desired.

How to make bracelets

STEP 1

Consider using elastic if you are a beginner. These sorts of bracelets are fun, and easy to make. You simply put the beads onto the cord and knot it. You do not need a clasp. To learn how to make a stretchy beaded bracelet, click here. You can buy beading elastic in a bead shop, or in the beading section of an arts and crafts store. Clear elastic thread comes in many different thicknesses. Thicker elastic is sturdy, which makes it suitable for large beads. Thinner elastic is more delicate, and looks best paired with smaller beads. Elastic cords have a thread or fabric covering. They are thick by beading standards, and usually come in black and white.

2
Try using wire if you are more advanced. Beading wire cannot be tied like elastic, and must be used with crimps and clasps. The crimps help hold the bracelet together. Be sure to use beading wire, which is flexible. Wire used for wire wrapping is too stiff and thick; it is not suitable for beading. To learn how to make a beaded bracelet with a clasp, click here.
Consider using memory wire for a fun, spiral bracelet.

3
Know that some beads work better with certain types of string. Smaller beads will work well on thin, delicate elastic. Large beads, however, will need something heavier, such as a thicker elastic or wire. You will also need to add extra length to your bracelet if you are using bulky beads. These beads fill up the space between the bracelet and your wrist, making the bracelet fit tighter.

4
Choose your beads. There are many different types of beads. Each material has a specific look, and some types of beads are more suitable to certain projects than others. Here are the most common beads you will find in bead shop or an arts and crafts store:
Plastic beads are the least expensive and come in many different shapes and colors. They are ideal for kids' arts and crafts. For a fun, kid-friendly bracelet, try using elastic cord in a bright color, and using plastic pony beads. You can also use alphabet beads so the kids can spell their names on the bracelet.

Glass beads are beautiful, and come in many different colors. They capture the light well and had a mid-price range. Most glass beads will be translucent, and some will have designs.

Semi-precious stones tend to be more expensive than glass beads. They also tend to be heavier. Because they are made from natural materials, no two beads are alike.

You can also find beads made from natural material, such as shell, wood, ivory, and coral. These tend to be expensive and unique; no two beads are the same.

5

Decide on a design before putting the beads on the elastic or wire. When buying beads, you may find that the beads are already strung for you. This is simply another way of packaging them, and is not suggestive of a final design. Simply snip the beads off their string and arrange them in a new pattern on your desk or bead tray. Here are some ideas for a design:

Put the largest beads towards the center, and the smallest beads towards the clasps.

Alternate large beads with smaller/spacer beads.

Use a warm (red, orange, yellow) or a cool (green, blue, and purple) color scheme.

Choose a bunch of beads that are all the same color, but in different sizes and shades. For example, you could use light blue, medium blue, and dark blue beads

STRETCHY BRACELETS

Equipment / Tools
Embroidery scissors
Bead stopper
Beading needles (collapsi by ble eye needle or big-eye needle)
Ruler or measuring tape

Materials
Seed beads
Stretch cord (such as Stretch Magic)

Cut a length of cord that is about 4 to 6 inches longer than your desired bracelet length. Affix a bead stopper about three inches from one end.

Pre-stretch the elastic cord by taking a length about three inches long and stretching lightly, move down and stretch the next section until you have pre-stretched the entire length. This will prevent your stretch bracelet from sagging.

This bracelet is made using a 0.5mm black stretch floss cord.

Unless your beads are large enough to string without a needle, thread a collapsible eye or big-eye needle onto the other end of the stretch cord and fold over a two-inch tail. This step is optional if you're using beads with very large holes; in that case, you can often string them directly onto the cord.

String all of the beads for your bracelet. Check the length occasionally by wrapping the strung beads around your wrist. Be sure to leave a little space between your skin and the bracelet, so that you can roll it over your wrist without breaking the stretch cord. This also helps to ensure that no empty areas show through. Make sure that the last bead you string has a hole large enough to hide a knot in your beading cord.

If you plan to make a stack of bracelets using the same beads, measure your strand now and jot down its length so that you can replicate it. If you make another bracelet using smaller or larger beads, you should check for fit with those because you may need the bracelet to be slightly shorter or longer.

When you are working with small beads like these that are all the same size, mixing in a few beads with a larger hole will make it easier for you to hide the knot.

Knotting your stretch bracelet takes the most practice. The ends can be slippery and the last thing you want is to drop the cord and see all those fabulous beads slide off the end.

For stacking seed bead bracelets, the square knot is best because it hides inside the beads better. With gemstone bracelets, use a surgeon's knot, as it is a little bulkier but more secure.

Remove the bead stopper and the needle from the elastic cord, and then bring both ends together. Carefully make the first half of a square knot, gently pulling the cord ends to remove slack in the bracelet.

While holding the first half of the knot in place, tie the second part of the knot and pull firmly to secure. It can be tricky at first to complete a knot without losing tension in the bracelet and allowing spaces to form between the beads. If you do lose tension, try pulling both ends of the cord away from each other to take up some slack. After completing a few bracelets, this should become much easier.

Some people use crimp beads rather than knots to secure the ends of the stretch cord. This method isn't recommended because the sharp metal edges of the crimps are likely to cut the cord.

While holding the bead away from your knot, apply a tiny drop of glue to the knot.
Let the glue dry before trimming the cord ends. This will make it less likely that the knot will loosen when you are trimming them.

Once the glue has dried, gently stretch out each cord end. Then, use embroidery scissors to trim the ends close to the beads.

CHAPTER 3

BAKING

baking, process of cooking by dry heat, especially in some kind of oven. It is probably the oldest cooking method. Bakery products, which include bread, rolls, cookies, pies, pastries, and muffins, are usually prepared from flour or meal derived from some form of grain.

Bread

There's nothing like taking a loaf of fresh yeast bread out of the oven. Just the enticing scent alone makes one of the world's most celebrated foods worth baking! From a handful of ingredients—at its most basic flour, yeast, water, and salt—to the finished product, learn all about the stages of bread baking here, including how to store your prized loaf. But some breads do not have yeast, such as flatbreads, and they, too, are discussed here.

Cakes

Layer cakes, cupcakes, snack cakes, roulades, and even cheesecakes—the cake category is vast. Most cakes are often classified into two categories: whether they contain fat, such as butter or oil (shortened cakes) or whether they contain little or no fat (unshortened or foam cakes). Find out more here about types of cakes, the ingredients used to make them, and plenty of tips for success.

Candy

Candy and confections range from chewy nougat and pralines to fudge, caramel, and toffee. The thing they share in common is sugar, and how that sugar is handled determines the category that candies fall into. There are essentially two categories of candies: crystalline or non-crystalline. Candies that are crystalline contain crystals in their finished form, like nougat and fudge, where as noncrystalline candies don't contain crystals (think lollipops and caramels).

Chocolate Confections

Chocolate is one of the most beloved ingredients in baking, and a true passion for many of us, especially when it comes to candy and confections. From cocoa to milk chocolate to bittersweet, understanding the different types of chocolate and when and how to use them can make or break your finished product. Find all this, along with how to melt and temper chocolate, and plenty of tips for success here.

Cookies

Whether you call them "cookies," "biscuits," or even "koekje," cookies are loved the world over. They can be dropped, sliced, molded, rolled and cut, baked into bars, sandwiched with fillings, and decorated with colorful icings. They can range from simple to elaborate, an after-school snack or essential to your family's holiday traditions.

Frosting, Icings, etc

Frostings, icings, fillings, buttercreams, and glazes all add a finishing touch to our baked goods, whether you are covering a carrot cake with a thick layer of cream cheese frosting, pouring chocolate glaze over a custard-filled layer cake, or coating cookies with lemon icing. Frostings, icings and buttercream are not only used to finish a dish but can be used as filling along with curds, custards, jam and whipped cream. Read more about the different types and when and how to use them here.

BAKING TOOLS FOR STARTING UP BAKING BUSINESS

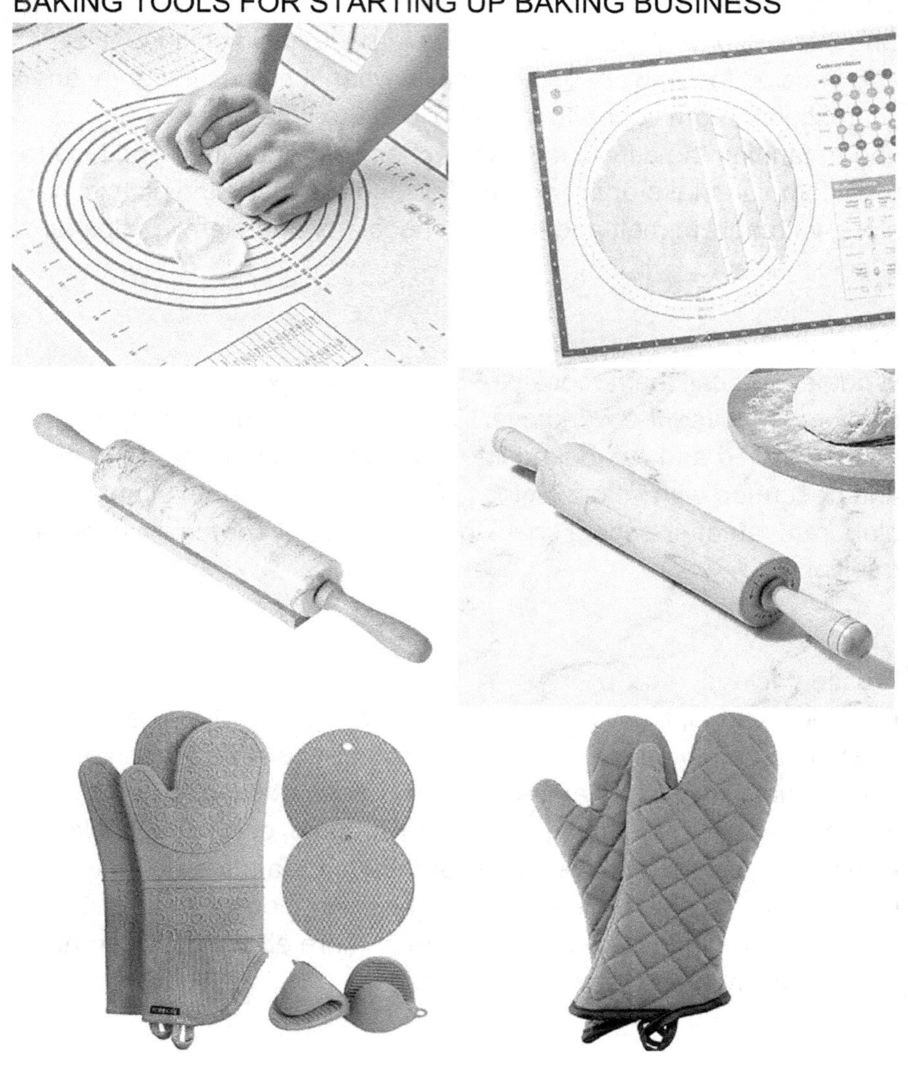

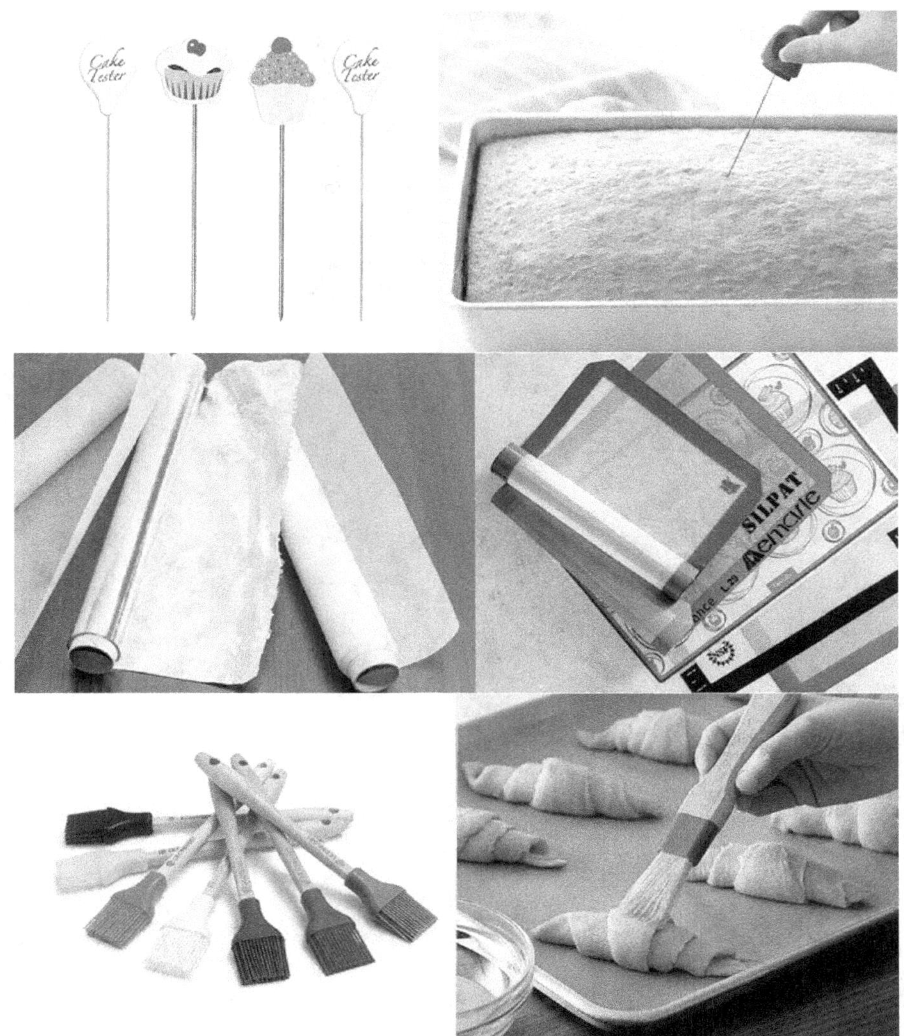

Above are some basic tools for baking.

SOME BASIC INGREDIENTS FOR BAKING

#1. Butter

There are several types of butter, but they are very expensive and scarce in the local market, but they can be found in the big supermarket. They are imported butter when used gives very good flavor and good results.

#2. Margarine

Margarine is the type that is found on the market and there are several types. This type of margarine is the best, it can give the best result in baking, for example. summer county, real vine margarine, etc.

1. Semi-good margarine: they are also good, but not like the previous ones, e.g topper, clematis, rose.

These are widely used in the country (NigeFAIRLY MARGARINE: These are the types of margarine that are not very good for baking, eg simas, turkey, blue stripe, etc. are not consistent, but are good for jollof rice.

#3. Granulated salt

While it probably seems obvious to always have salt in stock, this seasoning can make or break the balance and overall flavor of your baked goods, even when used in very small amounts.

Although the larger flake sea salt is not normally used for baking, it can be sprinkled over sweet and savory creations to add some texture and flavor.

#4. Granulated sugar

If you see the word "sugar" in a recipe, it generally refers to granulated sugar, the standard sweetener used to make almost any baked product.

As a general rule of thumb, granulated sugar should always be kept well-stocked in the pantry.

Dangote granulated sugar is the best sugar for baking right now. It is very necessary as a baker to have granulated sugar always.

#5. Yeast

Another form of yeast, yeast is a slow-growing agent that requires more time and patience than baking soda or powder.

Instant yeast and active dry yeast can be used to make bread slowly and steadily, allowing yeast cells to create carbon dioxide as they metabolize during kneading and standing periods.

#6. Cream of tartar

This acidic powder can be used in conjunction with baking soda to create a suitable environment to release carbon dioxide and make your baked goods rise.

There is no need to add cream of tartar when using baking powder as it already contains acid.

#7. Cornstarch

Some baked goods rely on this powder, which is typically used to thicken sauces and other recipes, to soften it, as it has the ability to neutralize the tough proteins in flour, making them softer.

#8. Flour

There are good and semi-good flours on the market for baking and they are

GOOD FLOURS: these are types of flour that are light and give good results, examples are Honeywell or supreme and supreme golden flour

ii. Semi-good-floor: not as good as Honeywell and supreme flour, eg. (golden penny), which is also better than Dangote flour. The reason this flour is not good is that it is stored for a long time. It hardens and has some insects.

#9. Baking Powder:

Baking powder is a leavening agent that makes your mixture rise, much of which makes the cake very dry.

#10. Eggs

Eggs are also a growth agent that makes a mixture to create.
It is advisable to use medium-sized eggs to bake cakes instead of large and small eggs to get an accurate measurement and always use fresh eggs.

#11. Cake Spices

There are several types of spices, eg cinnamon spices, nutmeg, etc. The most preferred type above is the cinnamon spice, but both can be combined to use in the cake mix.

#12. Flavors

There are many kinds of flavors and each one is suitable for a different mix, for example, we can combine some flavors for cake, except the lemon flavor because of its strong/strong flavor

(CAKE FLAVOR COMBINATION)

Strawberry / Butter Scotch

Vanilla Essence / Butter Scotch
vanilla/strawberry essence
Coconut / Butter Scotch
lemon/almond
#13. Dark Agent

Browning / Black Molasses / Cocoa Powder / Chocolate: These are all darkening agents, they are good but they last for a flavor that is bitter, so we need a sweetening agent for cakes to make the cake sweet, that's why the golden syrup is used as a sweetener.

#14. Cake Candy

Golden syrup is a sweetener for cakes, we use it in browning because of the bitter taste, there are some cakes that need golden syrup, they are cakes that crumble when cut. To avoid crumbling, you need golden to bind the cake mix.

#15. Fruits

These are dried fruits that contain several types of fruits, so they are called mixed fruits and before being used or placed in the cake mix they must be soaked in brandy

Why do people put fruit on a cake?

To make fruit soft
To make the fruit stay longer so as not to spoil (preservative), the fruit should be soaked in brandy for a period of 8 hours.
IF Cake Fruit Is Not Wet

The fruit will settle to the bottom of your mixture
The fruits will be hard and will spoil in time
#16. PRESERVER

Brandy There are several brands you can use, but the preferred types are 501, squadron, merit brandy e.t.c. they are placed or added to the cake mix before baking in the oven and also sprinkled on the cake after baking to keep it longer.
GOLD MIXTURE: Gold mix is a food-grade preservative, use to determine the long-standing preservative of your cake and other snacks
#17. Coasted chocolate

Whether you choose a variety of bittersweet chocolate, unsweetened, this ingredient is included in many heavy chocolate recipes, from melted dark chocolate cakes to chocolate pudding cakes.

Dark or sweet chocolate can also be used in place of chocolate chips in a recipe; just break it into small pieces for a more rustic touch.

This naturally sweet ingredient can be found in countless recipes and is a great way to add subtle flavor to a variety of baked goods like orange, sesame, and honey.

Jelly
No, we're not talking about the brightly colored sugary powders that come in gelatin packets, but the unflavored, sugar-free version, used to make creams, marshmallows, puddings, and more.

#18. Toasted chocolate

Whether you choose a variety of unsweetened, bittersweet, or sweet chocolate, this ingredient is included in many heavy chocolate recipes.

It can be used in place of chocolate chips in a recipe; just break it into small pieces for a more rustic touch.

#19. Flaked oats

This pantry staple is good for much more than oatmeal raisin cookies, and can be used to add texture to a variety of baked goods, from bread to muffins. Just make sure you're getting classic rolled oats, not instant.

#20. Cocoa powder

A key ingredient in any chocolate lover's pantry, cocoa powder is what's left after the cocoa butter is extracted from the beans, leaving only the bitter solids.

It's a necessary addition to most chocolates, and as a bonus, it's also said to have superfood benefits, so you can eat your cake and feel good about it, too.

#21. cream of tartar

This acidic powder can be used in conjunction with baking soda to create a suitable environment to release carbon dioxide and make your baked goods rise.

There is no need to add cream of tartar when using baking powder as it already contains acid.

#22. Cornstarch

Some baked goods rely on this powder, which is typically used to thicken sauces and other recipes, to soften it, as it has the ability to neutralize the tough proteins in flour, making them softer.

#23. Shortening

This shortening is sometimes used in place of or in addition to butter to create softer, more flexible baked goods, such as cookies and pie crusts, due to shortening's higher melting point.

#24. Pure vanilla extract

While you stock up, you can also buy some other pure extracts, like almond and lemon, for future baking efforts.

For those who want to take their vanilla game to the next level, whole vanilla beans can also be used to add a strong touch of flavor to their pasta and sauces.

#25. Icing sugar

This fine sugar is essential for making icings for cakes, cupcakes, and biscuits.

Let get in the business, first let's bake a Cake

HOW TO BAKE CAKE

This recipe makes a well risen 10 x 3 inch deep Cake.

500 grams(about 4 cups) Plain Flour /All purpose flour
500 grams Butter (at room temperature)
10 Eggs (at room temperature)
350 grams Sugar
2 tablespoonful Baking powder
2 tablespoonful flavor (coco or vanilla or butterscotch flavor)
1 cup Brandy or Rum(optional but most people add it)
2 tablespoonful Preservative powder (not necessary)(I don't use it
but most bakers do)
Half cup browning(for dark cakes) (optional)
1 handful Dry fruits (raisins, cherries) soaked in the alcohol you'll be
using(optional)
Notes:

– Preservative powder is necessary to extend the shelf life of the cake. It is best used for wedding and birthday cakes that need to be preserved in room temperature for some time before being coated with Fondant or icing. I always recommend freezing the cake instead of using preservatives.
The alcohol also helps to keep the cake from going stale.
– Browning is used for making dark brown cakes
(see how to make cake browning)
– Use fruits only if you want to make fruit cakes.
– 1 tablespoonful of Plain Flour is approximately 9 grams
– 1 tablespoon of sugar is approximately 13 grams
– I used oldenburger butter, you can get it all big supermarkets, like shop rite and Park n Shop, at the fridge section.

Steps

1. Sieve/sift the flour, baking powder and preservative(if you're using any) together in a wide bowl and set aside.

2. In a separate bowl or an electric cake mixer, cream the butter until it is light, fluffy and white, then add the
sugar and continue creaming until it goes from grainy to fluffy again.
Tips:The creaming step is very important in making Nigerian cake. This helps to trap enough air into the batter and also helps the cake gain additional volume and have a rich texture.
 If you're using an electric cake mixer, use the slow setting, so that the air bubbles can form slowly.

3. Add the eggs one after the other as you continue to cream.

4. Add the flavor, coloring, alcohol and soaked fruits.

5. Gradually add the flour mixture, one cup at a time.

Mix until well incorporated.

6. Pour the cake batter into the prepared cake pan and smooth the top with a spatula. The batter should fill the pan half way, if you have left over batter, you can pour it into another smaller pan.

7. Bake in the preheated oven (150°C or the 300°F) for 1 hour or until the cake is springy to the touch and has started to shrink out from the sides of the pans.
Some oven bake faster, while others are a bit slow, so check your cake after 45 minutes of placing it in the oven, to know if it is ready or needs further baking.
Cool the cakes in the pan for 10 minutes, then turn it onto a wire rack and leave to cool completely.

FONDANT ICING

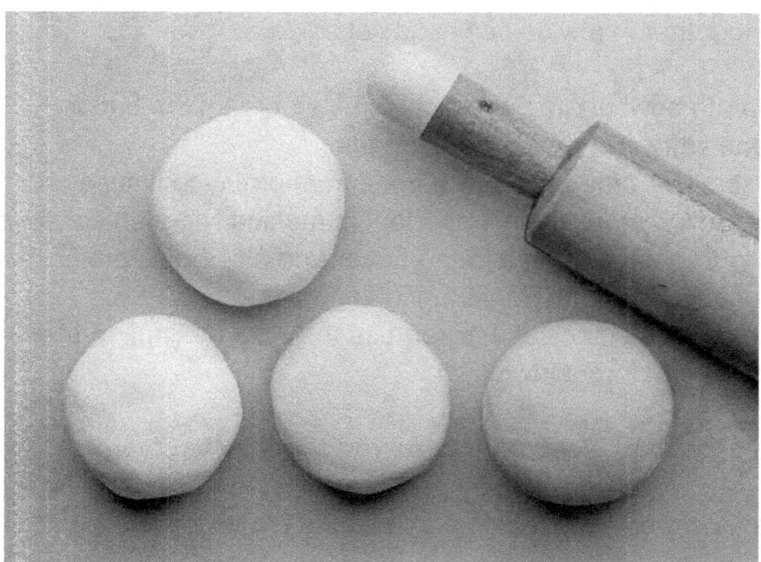

Consider the size of your cake

Ingredients
1.Lang sugar
2. Gelatin
3. Liquid glucose
4. Glycerin
5. Flavors
6. Corn flour
7. Rolling pin
8. Fonder cutter
9. Smoother
10. Water
11. Rolling board
12. Carbozine Maintain Glucose

Tips For Working with Rolled Fondant
It can dry out quickly. If you need to store it for short periods of time, wrap it in plastic wrap or cling wrap and store it in a resealable plastic bag.
For longer storage, roll it into a ball, then coat with a little vegetable oil. Wrap in plastic wrap, then place the wrapped fondant in an airtight container. It can be stored for up to 2 months this way. Do not refrigerate or freeze it.
If it is too soft or sticky to roll, knead in a little additional powdered sugar.
Make sure your hands are clean when handling, and avoid wearing clothing with fibers that might shed.
If you are covering a cake or cupcakes with rolled fondant, lightly cover with a glaze or buttercream frosting first to create a smooth surface.

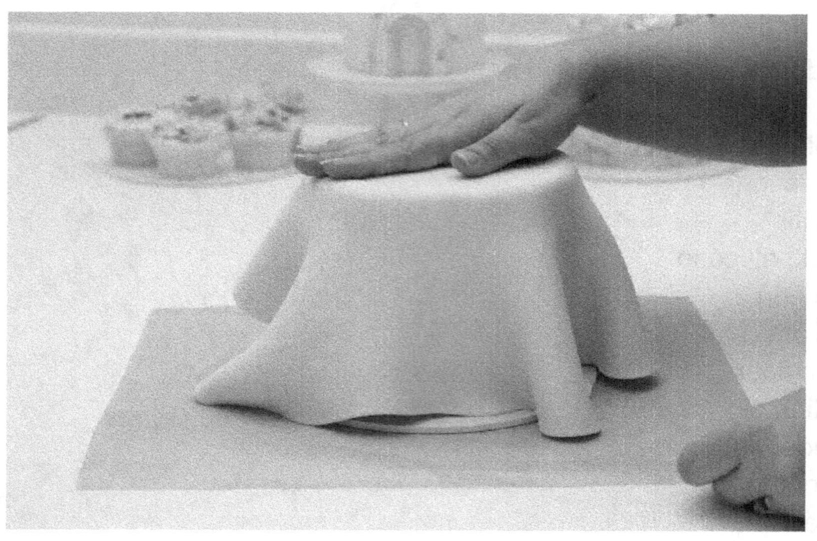

Instructions
Combine gelatin and cold water; let stand until thick. Place gelatin
mixture on top of double boiler and heat until dissolved.
Add glucose and glycerin, mix well. Stir in shortening and just before
completely melted, remove from heat and stir in vanilla. Mixture
should cool until lukewarm.
Place 4 cups of confectioners' sugar in a large bowl. Make a well in
the center and using a wooden spoon, stir in the lukewarm gelatin
mixture. Mix in sugar and add more a little at a time, until stickiness
disappears. Knead in remaining sugar. Knead until the fondant is
smooth, pliable and does not stick to your hands. If the fondant is
too soft, add more sugar; if too stiff, add water (a drop at a time).
IMPORTANT NOTE: IF YOUR FONDANT IS WET OR TOO SOFT
WHILE MIXING, ADD MORE SUGAR. IT CAN DIFFER
DEPENDING ON CLIMATE AND INGREDIENTS.
Use fondant immediately or store in an airtight container in the
fridge. When ready to use, bring to room temperature and knead
again until soft.

You can learn about bunch of snacks you can bake and sell to earn some extra cash

CHAPTER 4

FASHION

Clothing is a basic needs of Man. People need to cover their nakedness, be protected , adorned and admired by wearing apparels.Your clothings along with your grooming affects peoples judgments about you affects people's judgments. A person's first impression of you is based on your appearance. This gives the opportunity to enhance personal style in clothing.
The need to meet individuals need for Clothes necessitate changing form of clothing which is fashion
Fashion is anything currently in its applies to prevailing mode of expression that may or may not apply to everyone. Fashion covers more area than clothes such as fashion in hairstyle, home decoration, fabric Styling etc
Many years ago fashion changed very slowly but today fashion changes very quickly as a result of technological development

Fashion designing is the art of the application of designs, natural beauty aesthetics to clothing. This is influenced by social value, cultural and economic factors
Fashion designing involves creating and making clothing designs and accessories. A fashion designer is someone who creates apparel . Fashion designers studies about fashion trends sketch designs, select suitable materials for the production of clothes

Some basic tools for fashion designing

Sewing machine
Tailoring scissors
Pins / pincushion
Bobbin
Seam ripper
Iron / ironing board
Sewing Gauge
Tape
Needles
Paper and pencil
Thread
Zipper

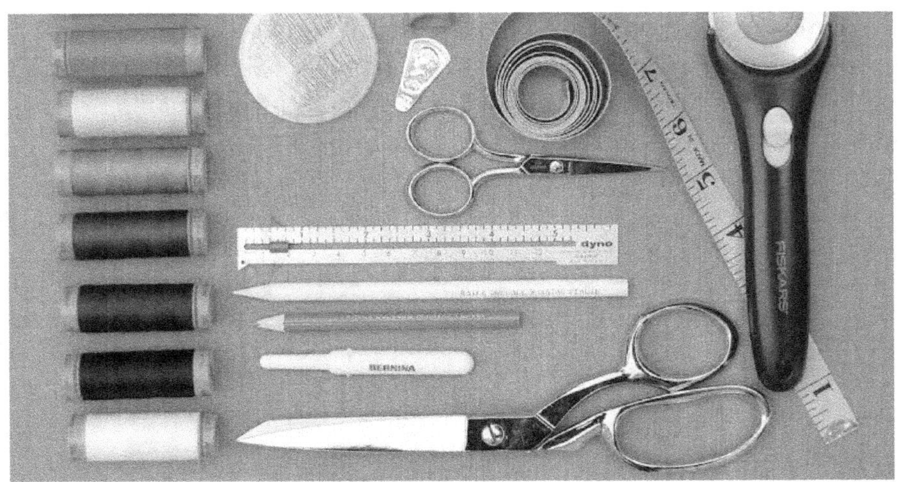

Learn the different tools you'll need. Making clothes requires a bunch of different tools for sewing, for making patterns, and for measuring the patterns to make sure that they will fit you. You will need to learn each type of tool and how to use it. In the beginning you won't be comfortable with all the tools, but the more you practice, the easier it will become.

Iron and ironing board. It's fine to use whatever quality iron you already have, but you'll probably want to eventually invest in a higher quality one. You'll be using the iron to press the item being sewn as you are sewing as this makes sure the seams stay open properly.

Seam ripper. You'll use this when you've made a mistake to rip out the wrong stitches.

Chalk for marking the fabric so you know where to sew and where to cut.

You'll need a really nice, sharp pair of scissors that you designate for cutting cloth only, otherwise the scissors will dull more quickly and can damage or fray your fabric.

Tracing paper for drafting your patterns and modifying the patterns as you're sewing.

Rulers for drafting and measuring while you're constructing your piece (both in the design stages and the sewing stages).

Tape measuring, especially a flexible tape measure. You'll use this to take measurements and make fit adjustments if you need them. Pins for holding the fabric in position before you start sewing. Pins should be used only sparingly as they can distort the fabric that you're working with.

Acquire a sewing machine. There are basically two types of sewing machines, ones that fall into the household/domestic category and ones that fall into the industrial use category. There are pros and cons to both of these categories so it will take a little deciding to figure out which will work best for your needs.[1]

Household sewing machines tend to be more portable and more versatile. They tend to do a variety of stitch types. However, they don't work out as well in terms of speed and power, and they aren't very good with heavy fabrics.

Industrial sewing machines are much more powerful and much faster, but they tend to only be able to do one type of stitch (such as a straight lockstitch). They do that one stitch very well, but aren't terribly versatile. They also tend to take up a lot more room.

If you want to sew stretchy materials, make sure your machine can do a zigzag stitch. Some machines have a specific stretch pitch, which is also helpful.

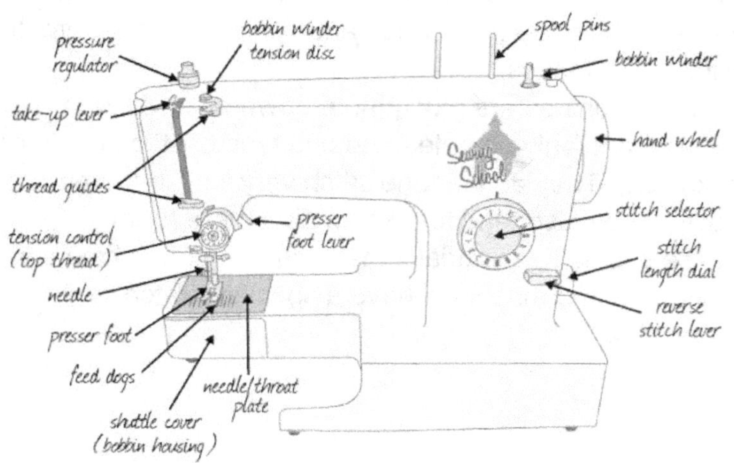

Learn the parts of your sewing machine. Hopefully your sewing machine will come with an instruction manual, because that will tell you which direction the bobbin is going to spin and where the bobbin case is. However, you're going to need to know at least the basic components of your sewing machine before you can get making fun things.

The spool holder holds the spool of thread and controls the direction of the thread while it goes through the sewing machine. Depending on the type of machine you have, your spool holder might be horizontal or it might be vertical.

Bobbin is basically a spindle that is wound with thread. You have to wind the bobbin with thread and fit it into the bobbin case (which is found under the needle plate).

Your sewing machine also has different stitch adjustments to help determine stitch length for each stitch, the amount of tension needed to make sure the stitches come through properly, and the different types of stitches (if you have the type of sewing machine that does different stitch types).

The take up lever controls the thread tension. If the thread tension isn't at its proper level the threads will knot up, jamming the sewing machine.

You can check with a nearby sewing shop to see if they have any classes or know anyone willing to help you get set up with your sewing machine, or you can ask a knowledgeable family member or friend.

Start simple. When you're just beginning with making clothes you'll want to start out with simple designs, otherwise it's easy to get frustrated and quit. It's best to start with skirts, because these are easier to make than say a 3-piece suit and they require you to take fewer measurements.

When you're first starting, try to avoid making clothes with buttons or zippers, like jackets. Do aprons or pajamas with elastic bands. Once you've gotten the hang of your tools and your sewing machine, then you can start advancing.

Make test garments. The best way to make your final piece the best it can possibly be is to make test clothes beforehand so you can tweak your design and make any changes to the final piece as you see fit.
It's recommended to use scraps from the same fabric as the final piece.
Make a dress for your little sibling

Factors to consider before sewing

1. Select the best fabric
2. Prewash fabric before sewing
3. Learn to cut fabric properly
4. Get a good enough sewing machine
5. Press as you sew
6. Always interface where necessary
7. Maintain your sewing machine
8. Learn to make clothes from sewing patterns
9. Get some nice sewing supplies and tools
10. Plan the sequence of stitching in advance
11.Always clip and trim seam allowances wherever necessary
12. Buy the best quality sewing notions and trims
13. Follow couture sewing techniques
14. Hang garments before hemming
15. Check for loose thread trails and trim away
16. Follow the Fitting standards in clothing

Start sketching.

Sketch [n.]: An outline or general delineation of anything; a first rough or incomplete draught or plan of any design; especially, in the fine arts, such a representation of an object or scene as serves the artist's purpose by recording its chief features; also, a preliminary study for an original work.
 Sketching means putting down your imagination on paper before it can be utilized

Sketching a blouse
- Draw the neck line
- Draw the shoulder,making it to slant or slope
- Draw the arms circle
- Draw the arm circle with a curve line, from shoulder point to slightly above bust line
- Draw a line from waistline to the hip line

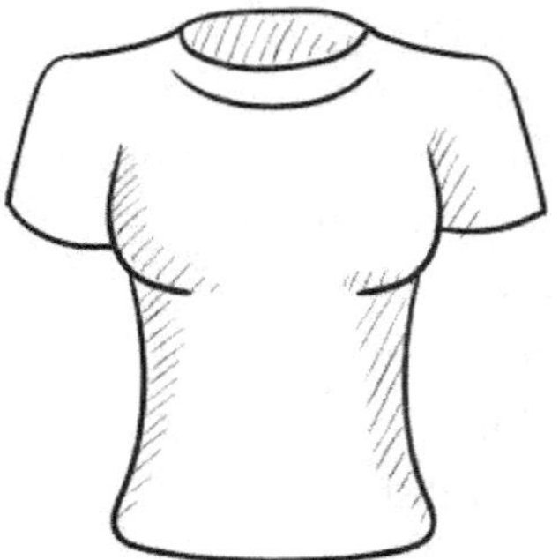

Dress

CHAPTER 5

HAIR DRESSING
Hairdressing is a lucrative business that can be done anywhere to
earn money, it's can be both professionally or side hustle
Hairdressing is one of the skills I will recommend people to acquire
Even as a student you can make hair for your fellow students for
money it's so good
Hairdressing is easy enough for everyone who puts interest in it. It
requires patience, determination and diligence

Hairdressing includes BARBING

Barber are hairdressers that specialize on cutting and maintaining hair and they often deal with men
Being a hairdresser provides a genuine opportunity to touch the lives of people in more ways than one. As a hairdresser, you influence your client's social life and shape part of their personality. A good look and a new feel could motivate them to look forward to their professional and social lives.

We can start with a simple style like cornrows

HOW TO MAKE CORNROWS

1.Wash and detangle your hair. Use your normal shampoo and conditioner to wash your hair. While its damp, detangle your hair with a leave-in conditioner and brush, then apply an oil or butter to lock in moisture. Your hair will be much easier to braid when it is moisturized and free of tangles.

Examples of oils or butters you can use to keep your hair moisturized and tangle-free are coconut oil, argan oil, jojoba oil, shea butter, or aloe butter products. Check the natural hair care aisle at a pharmacy or beauty supply store to find these products. If your natural hair is tightly coiled, you may also want to blow dry your hair before you start braiding. Blow drying will help stretch out your curls and give your cornrows a neater look.

2. Part your hair in rows from front to back. Use the end of a rat-tail comb to part your hair in rows from your forehead to the nape of your neck. You can part your hair down the middle first, from your forehead to your neck, then divide each side section into 1-3 more rows. Secure the rows in place with small-tooth clips or with bobby pins.

If you don't want a middle part, create 2 parts near the middle to make a row right on top of your head, then make more rows on the sides from there.

Try to make your parts evenly spaced so that your rows are about the same size.

3. Divide the first row into 3 small sections. Begin with a row of hair on top or on the side and unclip it. Take some hair in your fingers from the front near your forehead or ear. Separate that row into 3

even sections with your fingers: a left section, center section, and right section.[1]
You should use both hands to do this, with 1 hand holding 1 section of hair, while the other hand holds 2 separate sections of hair.
Before you start braiding, you may want to add a bit of edge control along your hairline. This will help you grip the hair easier, tame flyaways, and keep your cornrows neat.

4. Make the first braid stitch. Starting with either the left or right section in your fingers, move it over and on top of the center section, replacing the center with it. Then move the section on the opposite side over so that it is in the center, and switch the current centerpiece with that side.
At all times you will still have 1 hand holding 1 section of hair, while the other hand holds 2 separated sections.

5. Add a small section of hair from the row underneath to each braid stitch. Repeat the above braid stitch technique, adding a 1/2 in (1.3 cm) section of hair to each stitch as you go. Every time you make a new braid stitch, add more hair from the row, and continue until you reach the nape of your neck. This will keep the braid attached to your head.[2]
If you don't add more hair with each stitch, the braid will be loose and come out from your head instead of being in a cornrow style. Instead, you want to French braid each row.

6. Finish the braid once it's off your scalp and secure it with a hairband. When you get to your neck, you won't have any more hair to add into each stitch. Simply finish the braid until you've used up the rest of your hair. If you want, you can secure the braid when it's finished with an elastic hair band, rubber band, or small barrette.[3]
The length of the end of your braid will depend on how long your hair is.

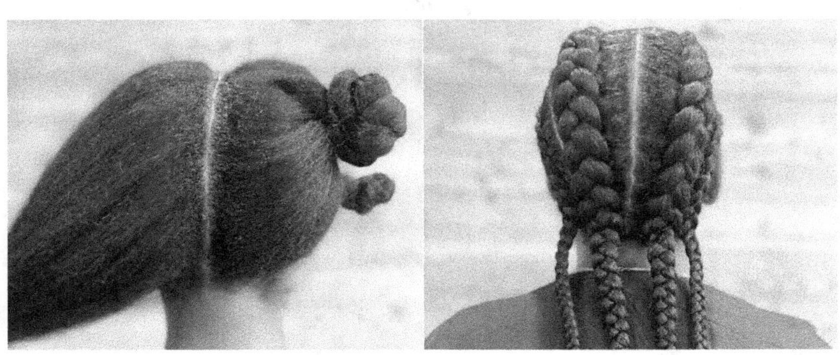

HOW TO MAKE PACKING GEL

 Different styles of packing gel you can make for your clients
You can start with

Hair tie and bobby pins
Wide-tooth comb
Hair brush
Hair gel
Spray bottle containing water

PROCEDURE

Spray your hair with water to moisten it just a little.
Use a wide-tooth comb to spread hair gel in a thin layer all over your
hair in upwards motions.

Repeat the same motions with a dense hair brush to distribute the hair gel all over your head, aiming for the top of your head.
Use a hair tie to secure the hair in a ponytail on top of your head.
Tame any stray hair strands with more hair gel or bobby pins.
You can leave the ponytail as it is, possibly decorating it with a nice scrunchie – it's one of the classic gel hairstyles. You can also twist your hair into an updo – in that case you'll need more bobby pins and possibly some hairspray to keep the bun as neat as possible.

NATURAL HAIR PACKING GEL
Hair Do packing gel?
Natural hair is the perfect hair for packing gel because it relaxes your natural hair and brings out the beauty in you. There are other hair extensions that can still serve. You do not only need your natural hair to achieve this.
What is the best gel for natural hair?
There are a lot of gels out there but which one is the best?. I suggest that if you are still asking this question you should try Mielle Organics Honey & Ginger Styling Gel. This is one get that will take you out of this planet, the way it relaxes your natural hair is another testimony for another day.
How do you make homemade gel?
Making homemade gel can be done in different ways. I suggest that beginners should try this simple process. Mix hot water and gelatin in a bowl, stir until it is properly dissolved.
What's the best hair gel for curly hair?
Ecoco Eco Styler Professional Styling Gel with Olive Oil is the best hair gel for curly hair, it settles the hair and prevents frizz. It gives the hair that perfect look that keeps you looking stunning all day long.

How long does hair gel last in hair?
It all depends on how you care for the hair when it is gelled up. Hair gel can last in hair up to 7days if you protect it well during the night.
Do you put gel in wet or dry hair
Application of gel on dry and dirty hair will make it less attractive. Do not totally dry up your hair, damp hair is the best hair to apply gel on.
What is the safest hair gel?
Aloe Vera content in a hair gel provides nutrients to a hair scalp. Jojoba Oil is a well known hair gel that is very safe. It helps bring back moisture to the hair.
What can I substitute for hair gel?
Gelatin hair mask and Aloe Vera gel can really serve as a substitute for hail gel. It has some natural content that can help relax your hair, provided that the hair is damp and clean.

CHAPTER 6

PHOTOGRAPHY

Photography is the art, application, and practice of creating durable images by recording light, either electronically by means of an image sensor, or chemically by means of a light-sensitive material such as photographic film.

The photography process can be broken into three distinct phases: planning, thinking, and execution.
Lines in photography are an immensely powerful element. Proper arrangement of lines, guides the eye around the image, often placing emphasis on the subject matter or conveying a sense of movement. Improper arrangement can draw the eye out of the photo or take away from the strength of the subject matter.

What is ISO in photography? ISO refers to your camera's sensitivity to light. The higher the ISO, the more sensitive your camera sensor becomes, and the brighter your photos appear. ISO is measured in numbers.

We have different types of photography

1. Portrait Photography

One of the most common photography styles, portrait photography, or portraiture, aims to capture the personality and mood of an individual or group. Images may be candid or posed, full body or close-ups. Either way, the subject's face and eyes are typically in focus. Lighting and backdrop help to convey tone and emotion. Popular types of photography portraits include senior portraits, family portraits, engagement photos, and professional headshots. The best portrait photographers make clients feel completely comfortable, so that their expressions are natural and relaxed.

2. Photojournalism

Photojournalism is a way of telling the story of a newsworthy (perhaps even historic) event or scene through photographs. Photojournalism should be as objective and truthful as possible and capturing candid moments as they happen is more important than getting picture-perfect shots. Generally, photojournalists attend planned events with the hope of capturing unplanned, unscripted moments. Their work is routinely published in magazines and newspapers.

3. Fashion Photography

Fashion photography showcases and glamorizes fashion clothing, shoes, and accessories to make them more desirable to consumers. It is commonly published in magazines and online. People may choose this niche over different types of photography because of the opportunity to be highly creative in making photographs eye-catching and appealing. Fashion photographers take a lot of full body shots and work in an array of locations, from fashion shows to studios with full lighting setups to city streets and open fields. They utilize many of the same skills as portrait photographers and must practice good teamwork and communication when working with shoot stylists, creative directors, and models.

4. Sports Photography

By catching athletes, coaches, and even fans at the perfect moment, sports photographs can depict the passion, drama, and emotion that fuels sporting events. Sports photographers must aim and shoot quickly to keep up with the action around them, and it's best practice to use a higher ISO to shoot at a faster shutter speed. Sports photographers also usually use long, heavy lenses for zooming in on the action. Interesting angles can help make your work stand out in this competitive genre.

5. Still Life Photography

Like it sounds, still life photography features inanimate objects—natural or manmade. Still life photography can be artistic or commercial. It is commonly used in stock photography as well as product advertising. (Think of the product images shown in catalogs, magazines, and billboards.) For still life photographers, object selection, arrangement, and lighting are key to getting a great shot.

6. Editorial Photography

Editorial photography is taken to illustrate a story or article, typically for a magazine or newspaper. The subject of editorial photography can vary widely and is entirely dependent on the topic of the text it accompanies. Generally, for editorial photography, you'll want to get shots that work for a variety of layouts, including horizontal and vertical compositions. When working in editorial photography, you are likely to work closely with writers and art directors, and demonstrating good communication skills and professionalism will help you succeed.

7. Architectural Photography

Both the interior and exterior design of buildings and structures are the subject of architectural photography. From warehouses to city bridges to old country barns, this genre encompasses diverse structures. Often, the photograph showcases the structure's most aesthetically pleasing parts, such as a particular beam or archway. Interesting materials and colors may also be emphasized. Lighting can be challenging in architectural photography and, for exteriors, photographers must know how to work with natural light. Gear such as a tilt-shift lens, a tripod, and a panorama head is often useful. Architectural photographs can be of value to designers, architects, leasing companies, and building investors.

HOW TO START PHOTOGRAPHY

1. Learn to hold your camera properly
2. Start shooting in RAW
3. Understand the exposure triangle

4. Wide aperture is best for portraits
5. Narrow aperture is best for landscapes
6. Learn to use Aperture Priority and Shutter Priority modes
7. Don't be afraid to raise the ISO
8. Make a habit of checking the ISO before you start shooting
9. Be careful with your on-camera flash
10. Learn to adjust white balance
11. Learn to read the histogram
12. Play with perspective
13. Understand the rule of thirds
14. Eyes should always be in focus
15. Pay attention to the background
16. Invest in a tripod
17. Shoot in the early morning and evening
18. Invest in some good photo editing software
19. Be selective
20. Learn from your mistakes

EQUIPMENT FOR PHOTOGRAPHY

- Camera

- Tripod

- Lighting

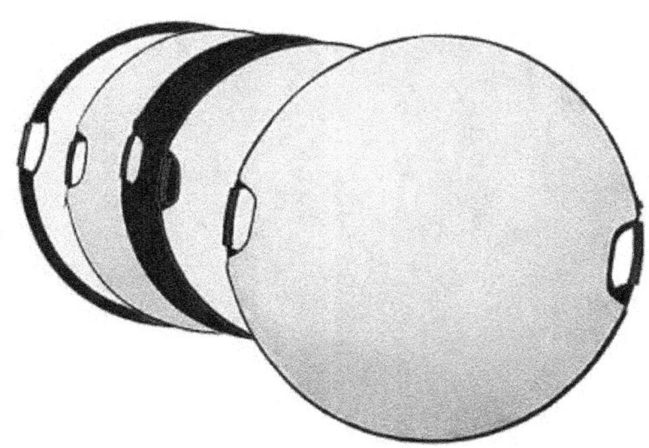

- Lenses

- Backdrop

- Computer

- An Editing software

Adobe Lightroom
Photo Editor & Picture Presets
(123k)
GET

Adobe
Sign In

Photo editing made for everyone.
Free trial
Buy now

How to edit a photo with online Photoshop tools in Adobe Express.

1: Upload your photos.
Upload your image from your own photo library or select a stock image to feature in your design. Select a single image or choose multiple photos to create a photo collage—don't worry, even in photo collages, you'll be able to edit each photo individually.

2: Adjust your images.
Select the photo to access the editing menu options. Under the Filters tab, you can add depth and style with preset filters. The Enhance option helps you finetune your photos with sliders for contrast, brightness, saturation, warmth, or sharpening. Play with the Blur effect for transforming your image, and pair it with the Remove Background tool to create perspective. Lastly, explore with Crop & Shape to rotate, scale, nudge, or flip your photo until the perfect composition is achieved.

3: Resize your photos.
Once you've reached the perfect edit for your photo or design, choose the Resize tool and a world of photo formatting options is at your fingertips. Select from social post sizes, social media profile photo sizes, print options, and other standard photo sizes. Adobe Express is your one-stop-shop for resizing your images, from Instagram and LinkedIn to your block party poster or holiday greeting card.

4: Add text to your photos.
Make photos pop with fabulous fonts, special effects, and color palettes. Our photoshop online tools let you customize everything: size, alignment, text box opacity, a vast selection of fonts, and bold color palettes that play to your design's aesthetic. Add text animation for extra pizazz with this online alternative to Photoshop.

5: Apply photo animations to your design.
You can also incorporate animation with the photos in your design.
From the animation menu, scroll past the text options until you
reach the photo animation effects. Play around with the featured
options until you find an animation effect that brings your design to
life.

6: Add animated stickers.
We've teamed up with GIPHY to offer you an ever-evolving library of
animated stickers. Adding a moving sticker or GIF to your Adobe
Express design is the easiest way to transform a graphic into an
animated social video.

7: Explore different design styles.
Adobe Express is a treasure trove of creative resources. Get
suggestions on design options, layouts, color, alignment and
animation, so you're never alone.

8: save, download and share.
Instantly download your edited image to your device. Share it across
your social channels and digital platforms, or print it out at home, at
work, or with a professional printer. Adobe Express saves your
designs so you can always go back and make additional changes.
Undo any changes you don't like as you go. No edits are
permanent, so you can always revert to your original version as
needed.